GIRAFFES

AFRICAN ANIMAL DISCOVERY LIBRARY

Lynn M. Stone

Rourke Corporation, Inc.
Vero Beach, Florida 32964

PHOTO CREDITS

All photos by the Author

LIBRARY OF CONGRESS
Library of Congress Cataloging-in-Publication Data
Stone, Lynn M.
  Giraffes / by Lynn M. Stone.
  p. cm. — (African animal discovery library)
  Summary: Describes the physical characteristics, habitat, and
behavior of the giraffe.
  ISBN 0-86593-050-3
  1. Giraffe—Juvenile literature. [1. Giraffes.] I. Title.
II. Series: Stone, Lynn M. African animal discovery library.
QL737.U56S76   1990
599.73'57—dc20   89-48442
                           CIP
                           AC

Portrait of giraffe

TABLE OF CONTENTS

THE GIRAFFE

Imagine being so tall that you have to bend over to nibble on tree leaves!

The giraffe *(Giraffa camelopardalis)* is that tall. Giraffes often dip their necks down to browse on leaves with their long tongues.

How tall is a giraffe? Most giraffes are between 14 and 18 feet tall. One giraffe, however, reached 20 feet. That is twice as tall as the rim of a basketball hoop.

Giraffe

THE GIRAFFE'S COUSINS

No other mammal is quite like a giraffe. The giraffe is easily the tallest mammal in the world.

Still, the giraffe does have a close cousin, the okapi. The okapi also lives in Africa.

The okapi doesn't have a giraffe's spots or its long neck. Its body, head, teeth, and long tongue are similar to a giraffe's.

An okapi stands about six feet tall and weighs about 550 pounds.

Giraffe family

HOW THEY LOOK

Everyone knows the giraffe by its big brown spots and its long neck. That amazing neck has the same number of bones as your neck—seven. But they are spaced far apart.

Both male and female giraffes have four small horns. They grow in two pairs, and they are covered by skin and hair. No other animal has horns like a giraffe's.

The giraffe has large, heavy feet and large eyes and ears. The average adult giraffe weighs nearly 1800 pounds.

Giraffes on savanna

WHERE THEY LIVE

The whole area in which an animal lives is called its **range.** The giraffe's range includes large sections of Africa south of the Sahara Desert.

Most giraffes live on **savannas** in central and eastern Africa. An African savanna is land that is covered mostly by grass but with patches of trees. Giraffes especially like savannas with thorny acacia trees.

Giraffes feeding

Giraffe with zebras

HOW THEY LIVE

Giraffes like each other's company. They are usually together in groups of two to six. Large groups, or **troops,** of giraffes may have as many as 70 animals.

Giraffes can gallop at nearly 35 miles per hour. They generally travel at a slow pace, however, feeding mostly in the early morning and late afternoon. They stand in the shade during the heat of the day and rest at night.

Giraffes sometimes cough, snort, or bellow.

Giraffe grazin

THE GIRAFFE'S BABIES

A mother giraffe usually has one baby, or **calf.** She rarely has twins.

A mother giraffe has her calves about a year and one-half apart. A giraffe calf weighs between 100 and 150 pounds at birth, and it already stands nearly six feet tall.

A giraffe grows for 10 years. Giraffes may have their own babies before they reach full adult size.

Giraffes in zoos have lived to be 28 years old. It is unlikely that wild giraffes live that long.

Baby giraff

PREDATOR AND PREY

Giraffes are plant eaters, or **herbivores.** They live on a diet of leaves, leaf buds, fruit, grass, melons, corn, and other plants.

A giraffe has a hard time drinking or eating off the ground. It must spread its front legs widely or bend to its knees.

Like other herbivores, giraffes may become food, or **prey,** for fierce, hunting animals called **predators.**

Healthy, adult giraffes are too big and fast to be caught by most predators. Giraffes have a mighty kick, too. But baby giraffes are often hunted by lions.

frican lion

GIRAFFES AND PEOPLE

Many people visit Africa to see the remarkable animals there. The giraffe is a favorite.

Some of the native people of Africa kill giraffes for their skin, or **hide.** The hide is dried and made into leather. The leather is used for musical instruments, the strings of bows, shields, and clothing.

When people from Europe began to settle Africa, they killed great numbers of giraffes. They also used the hides.

Giraffes are sometimes used for food. The meat is tasty but tough.

Baby giraffe nursing

THE FUTURE OF GIRAFFES

All of Africa's large animals face a difficult future. As Africa's human population grows, animal homes are changed into cities and farms.

Already, the range of the giraffe has shrunk. The only large population of giraffes now is in the country of Tanzania and in nearby areas.

Wild giraffes in the future will probably live only in Africa's parks and reserves. Reserves are places that are protected from hunting and building.

Glossary

calf (KAF)—the baby or young of a giraffe or of several other large, hoofed mammals

herbivore (ERB a vore)—an animal which eats plants

hide (HIDE)—an animal's skin

predator (PRED a tor)—an animal that kills other animals for food

prey (PREY)—an animal that is hunted by another for food

range (RAYNGE)—the entire area in which a certain type of animal lives

savanna (sa VAN nuh)—broad, grassy areas with few trees

troop (TROOP)—a group of certain animals, such as giraffes

INDEX